To Ruth

Harvey Hirsch

PALE
MOON

Other Books by Harvey Hirsch

A HOME FOR TANDY*
(Platt & Munk)
(with Audrey Hirsch)

THE CRÈCHE OF KRAKOW, A Christmas Story**
(Momentum Books, Ltd.)
(with Audrey Hirsch)

BARBED WIRE And Other Pointed Remarks
(Cobblestone Press)

PALE MOON, Selected Poems
(Cobblestone Press)

*Republished in THE PLATT & MUNK TREASURY OF STORIES
FOR CHILDREN (Grosset & Dunlap)

**Reissued as GRANDMA'S LOST GIFT (Cobblestone Press)

PALE MOON

SELECTED POEMS AND PROSE VIGNETTES

BY
HARVEY HIRSCH

COBBLESTONE PRESS
A Division of Cobblestone Books, Inc.
Ann Arbor, New York, London

COBBLESTONE PRESS
A Division of Cobblestone Books, Inc.
Ann Arbor, New York, London

Copyright ©2002 by Harvey Hirsch

All rights reserved under International and Pan-American
Copyright Conventions. Published by Cobblestone Press,
a Division of Cobblestone Books, Inc.
Distributed in the United States by Cobblestone Books, Inc.,
Ann Arbor, Michigan.

A number of the poems in this work were originally published, some in
different form, in various literary journals and reviews. Permission to
reprint them here has been obtained. No part of this publication may
be reproduced or transmitted in any form or by any means, electronic or
mechanical, including photocopy, recording, or any information retrieval
system, without permission in writing from the publisher. Requests for
permission to make copies of any part of this work should be obtained
from the Copyrights and Permissions Department of Cobblestone Press,
a Division of Cobblestone Books, Inc.

Library of Congress Cataloging-In-Publication Data
Hirsch, Harvey [Date]
PALE MOON: Selected Poems/Harvey Hirsch
I. Title
1. United States - Poetry
PS3558.I77 P35 2002
811'.54 — dc20
98-93510 CIP
1st ed. p.   cm.
ISBN: 0-929613-01-5

Designed by Rebecca Waske
Manufactured in the United States of America
Acid-Free Paper

FIRST EDITION
02 03 04 05 06 • 5 4 3 2 1

Pale moon,
Held in the
Black arthritic fingers
Of winter trees.

— *from "Phases Of The Moon"*
PALE MOON

CONTENTS

PROLOGUE

November	1
Are We Lost Among the Stars?	2

I
AMONG THE STARS

When I Look Upon The Heavens	3
Here We Are Among The Stars	4
Reflections	5
Phases Of The Moon	5
Sun Cycle	7
Suspended In The Void Of Space	8
While He Reaches For The Stars	9
Someday, They Say	10
How The Universe Came To Be	11
The Starlight In Your Hair	13
Life Is Like A Shooting Star	13
Arabian Nights	14

II
EARTH, SEA, AND SKY

The Eagle	15
The River	15
The Thrasher	16
Spring Wakes Us	17

At The Lake	18
Mountains	19
Thus May The Darkness	19
Wind	20
Spring	21
I Like A Day	21
Summer Nights	22
Sitting Under An Apple Tree	22
Year Round	23
But I Don't Know Why	23
Hidden Lake	24
Jay	26
Robin	26
Above Me, The Sky Was Empty	27
Indian Summer	28
The Seasons	28
Late Autumn	29
But Now It Makes No Sense	30
Sing A Song	31
Profit Is The Benediction	32
The Earth We Despoil	32
Midwinter's Eve	33
A Solitary Bird	33
In The Middle Of The Night	34
In The Woods	35
The Flowers Of Our Dreaming	36
I Watched The Hawk	37

Whodunit	37
Regatta	38
The Flying Fish	38
Oh, What A Varied Place Is Earth	39
Jaguar	39
And, Once Again . . .	40
Little Things	41
Every So Often	42

III
PAST, PRESENT, FUTURE

Apartment 5B	43
Choices	43
The City	44
Upon This Field	46
What Man Has Done To Man	47
Having Enemies	47
Joe's Bar	48
To Be Thoroughly Fit	49
Life	49
Music	50
Madam Sophia	53
Audrey Rose	54
A Subtle Magic	55
The Drunkard's Tale	56
Are You Getting Anywhere?	57
On First Looking Into *Hawley's Chemical Dictionary*	58

Listen	59
Fanatics	59
History	59
Blow The Bugle	60
Glory Is For The Living	61
The Battle Flags Were Raised On High	62
I Wonder	66
There Was A Tapping At My Window	67
There Is A Road	69
Lost And Alone	70

IV
NIGHTFALL

Often, At Nightfall	71
They Sat Alone	72
What Shall I Say?	76
On The Windswept Prairie	76
Winter	77
And Dream That I Am There	80
Oh, When Did I Grow Old?	81
Harriet Green	82
When The World Was Six Years Old	84
Yesterday	85
Oh, Jenny, She Loved Me	86
Sweet Marie	86
Oh, My Darling Little Girl	87
Alas, That Time Has Come To Me	88

The Sand Is Falling In The Glass	88
A Very Long Time Ago	89
You And Me	89
Mirror Image	90
"Poor Old Thing . . ."	91
Do Not Think About The Winter	94
Of All Life's Treasures	94
Deep In The Still And Silent Night	95
And Now, There She Sat	96
And Yet, The Night Will Surely Come	98
There Is A Moment	99
Alone	100
Dusk	100

V
DUST

No Matter	101
I Think Of You	102
The Promise Of The Dawn Has Fled	104
Love Is Like A Flower	104
The Perfect Clock	105
Day By Day	105
But I Cannot Tell You Why	106
And So Did He	107
I've Watched The Seasons Come And Go	108
Memories	109

The Memory Of You	109
Life And Death	110
Roses	111
Courtship And Marriage	111
In The Darkening Gloom Of Evening	112
The Game Of Life	112
What Is Man?	113
A Most Valuable Lesson	113
Though One Be A King	114
Old Men	115
I Miss You So	116
In The Merry Month Of May	118
She Loved Me, She Said	118
If You Were Here	119
The First Time I Saw You	120
Mai Ling	122
Swan Queen	123
Being Dead's An Awful Bore	124
And Yet . . .	126
When The Bells Will Toll For Thee	127
Winter's Come	127
Dust	128

EPILOGUE

Upon The Beach	129

PROLOGUE

NOVEMBER

Late afternoon, a sunless, slate-gray sky casts a pale half-light
over the old mountains of worn, eroded rock, and on the
surrounding hills, covered with dense stands of towering hemlock,
pitch pine, and leafless maple, hickory, and black oak, through
which countless brooks and creeks snake their way along
toward still larger rivulets and streams.

Thin, ragged clouds of low-hanging fog slowly and silently fill
the narrow hollows between the dark, heavily wooded hills,
followed by a cold, drizzling rain that sweeps across the
empty fields, watering the lifeless yellow-gray weeds that
stand stiffly at field's edge, beneath the curled and rusted
wire fencing that hangs from old blackened fenceposts.

All is silent, except for the patter of the rain against a metal
roof and the tapping of a broken shutter, swinging slowly in
the cold, wet wind that blows through the bare branches and
along a narrow, unpaved and puddled road that curves around
a low rise, then descends and disappears into the deepening
shadows and intense darkness of the woods.

The sun sets and the hills and hollows are engulfed in darkness,
while a small pale moon rises slowly through the stiff, silhouetted
branches of the leafless trees — there is an intense stillness
and silence, except for the pattering of the rain against the
metal roof and the tapping of the broken shutter, hanging
from a rusted hinge.

Above, in the intense blackness of the night sky, the moon
glows dimly through ragged windswept clouds that drift slowly
toward the distant hills — and there, beyond the hills, beyond
the mountains, beyond the moon itself, are the stars — tiny
diamond-like glints of light, shimmering coldly in the infinite
blackness of the night.

ARE WE LOST AMONG THE STARS?

Are we lost among the stars,
Propelled by some cosmic force,
Spinning on through endless space
On a dark and wandering course?

We do not know where Earth is bound,
Which star is the light to trust,
Or if we'll travel on forever
Through clouds of cosmic dust.

We do not know what lies beyond
The outer reach of space,
Or if the darkness ever ends
In some far and distant place.

We do not know from where we came,
Or what the stars portend,
We do not know how it all began,
Or how it all will end.

We do not know, yet travel on,
Wherever Earth is bound,
And dream someday we find our way,
And Paradise is found.

I
AMONG THE STARS

WHEN I LOOK UPON THE HEAVENS

When I look upon the heavens
on clear and starry nights,
I know that Earth is but a speck
among a billion twinkling lights.

And I wonder if we're all alone
and will it always be,
Alone forever on a speck of dust
in a minor galaxy.

Is there not a single world
among those points of light,
That fill the farthest depths of space
and light the starry night?

And is our tiny voice not heard
when we call out in the night?
Is there really no one there
on some distant point of light?

Oh, I feel so lost and lonely
on clear and starry nights,
To think that we are all alone
among a billion twinkling lights.

But then I think about your touch,
and the joy that I have known,
And the night is alive with love and light,
and I know I'm not alone.

HERE WE ARE AMONG THE STARS

Here we are among the stars
On a tiny ball of clay,
And round a burning ball of fire
We spin both night and day.

And round, and round, and round we go,
Spinning night and day,
An endless journey round a star
On a tiny ball of clay.

And when I'm asked just why we spin,
I know not what to say,
Except that we shall spin forever
On a tiny ball of clay.

And round, and round, and round we go,
Spinning night and day,
An endless journey among the stars
On a tiny ball of clay.

And when I'm asked where we are bound,
I know not what to say,
Except that we shall spin forever
On a tiny ball of clay.

And round, and round, and round we go,
Spinning night and day,
An endless journey, I know not where,
On a tiny ball of clay.

REFLECTIONS

Golden
Stepping
Stones
Across
The
Undulating
Blackness
Of
The
Sea

Pathway
To
The
Moon
·

PHASES OF THE MOON

Pale moon,
Held in the
Black arthritic fingers
Of winter trees.

—

Silver moon,
Sailing through
Translucent mists
Of windswept clouds.

—

Ocean moon,
Viewing her golden
Reflection in the
Broken mirror
Of the sea.

—

Crescent moon,
Shy and retiring,
Hiding her pale beauty
Behind the dark velvet
Curtain of the night,
Showing only the arc
Of one lighted cheek.

—

Jungle moon,
Surprised at seeing her
Golden image reflected in the
Startled and staring eyes
Of a wakened jaguar.

—

Urban moon,
Dull lamp
Above the bright lights
And stone-filled shadows
Of the city.

—

Harvest moon,
Floating fat and full
Above the frozen stubble
Of autumn fields.

—

Full moon,
Night light
For a sleeping city.

—

Cold moon,
Pale and impassive,
Silent watcher
Over the vast emptiness
Of our lives.

SUN CYCLE

Rising sun,
Swelling with fire and light,
Melting the blackness
Of the fast retreating night.

—

Noonday sun,
Floating fat and free
Above the moist green fields
And glistening sea.

—

Setting sun,
Slipping slowly out of sight
Beneath the thick dark
Blanket of the night.

SUSPENDED IN THE VOID OF SPACE

Suspended in the void of space,
Upon this spinning sphere,
I do not know from where we came,
Or if anyone knows we're here.

And when I look upon the stars,
And the night is cold and clear,
I wonder if, among the stars,
Anyone knows we're here.

And when we feel that we are lost,
And when we cry in fear,
I wonder if, in another place,
Anyone knows we're here.

And when we grow too old for hope,
And we are in despair,
Will anyone hear our cries of pain?
And will anyone really care?

But then I feel you close to me,
And I know I need not fear,
For when I hear you speak my name,
I know *you* know I'm here.

WHILE HE REACHES FOR THE STARS

Mortal man's a contradiction,
It's in his genes and in his blood,
That while he reaches for the stars,
His feet tread in the mud.

For on this tiny ball of clay
That spins forever round the sun,
One can see the awful horror
Of the evil man has done.

And though he yearns to reach the stars
To free him from the mud,
Here on Earth are war and death
And his hands are stained with blood.

Oh, mortal man's a contradiction,
It's in his genes and in his blood,
That while he reaches for the stars,
His feet tread in the mud.

SOMEDAY, THEY SAY

Someday, they say, the sun will swell
And grow to twice its size,
And melt the polar icecaps
And cause the seas to rise.

The heat, they say, will boil the seas
And melt our ball of clay,
And then the sun will burst apart
And that will end the day.

And though there's still a little while
Before this doom arrives,
It might be wise to think about
How we should spend our lives.

So think about the future
And man's inexorable fate,
And raise your glass to love and life
Before it grows too late.

But do not fear, the end's not near,
We need not shed our tears,
There still is time for love and wine . . .
We've got a billion years!

HOW THE UNIVERSE CAME TO BE

Oh, I've tried to fathom the mystery
Of how the universe came to be,
Of how the endless dark of night
Was filled with countless points of light,
And I've wondered if the void of space
Was once a dark and empty place,
And if there is an end to space
Where light and time have left no trace,
Or if the stars are in a race
To reach the farthest depths of space.
Yes, I've tried to fathom the mystery
Of how the universe came to be,
Of how the endless dark of night
Was filled with countless points of light.

From where, I wondered, did all this come,
And how, I wondered, was all this done,
And did the billions of burning stars,
The quarks, the quasars, the planet Mars,
Come from some colossal bang —
Was there some stupendous clang —
That rang throughout all endless space
And set in motion an endless race
To the farthest reaches of deepest space
To fill the void and every place
With a boiling shower of glowing gases
That clumped together in molten masses
To form the stars and all we see,
The comets, the planets, the galaxy?

Oh, how I'd dearly love to know
What made this glorious cosmic show
And made the heavens to sparkle so,
The stars to twinkle, the moon to glow,
And filled the void with moons and Mars,
With planets and galaxies and shooting stars,
With particles and rays and asteroids,
That fill the farthest, deepest voids,
And countless, countless points of light,
All burning in the dark of night,
Burning and spinning with astral light,
Great wheels of fire burning bright,
Billions of stars and points of light,
All speeding away into endless night.

Oh, yes, I've tried to fathom the mystery
Of how the universe came to be,
But the answer, I find, is where none can go,
There simply is no way to know,
And so I am content to be
A product of this mystery,
A simple watcher of the skies,
And though I may not win a prize
For solving all the mysteries
That man has pondered for centuries,
I'll simply marvel at the show
Of countless stars that sparkle and glow,

That fill the mind and move the heart
With ancient light from worlds apart,
But though I say I do not know
How came this glorious cosmic show,
How came this endless sea of lights
That light the deepest darkest nights,
I know that I will always be
So grateful that there's you and me . . .
But that's another mystery!

THE STARLIGHT IN YOUR HAIR

Long I searched the stars for answers,
But the answers were not there,
And then, at last, I found them all,
In the starlight in your hair.

LIFE IS LIKE A SHOOTING STAR

Life is like a shooting star
That streaks across the skies,
It burns intensely for a little while,
Then fades away and dies.

ARABIAN NIGHTS

Once, long ago, before the beginning of time, when
towering giants ruled the Earth, they cast
great treasures of precious jewels and gemstones
into the sky, where they could be seen glittering
and twinkling in the blackness of the night.

Great handfuls of sparkling white diamonds,
luminescent pearls, and glittering gemstones of
blue, pink, and violet sapphires, blood-red
rubies, saffron-colored opals, and dark green
emeralds, were thrown with wild abandon
into the sky, all trembling, twinkling, and
glowing with fire and light in the blackness
of the night.

Sudden flashes of firelight streak across the sky,
bright glints of silver and gold from the burnished
blades and hilts of curved daggers and scimitars, and
jewel-encrusted scabbards, that glow and burn in
the blackness of the night.

And dominating all, a great white luminescent ball of
glowing moonstone, hanging cold and motionless in
the infinite blackness of the night.

While here, below, a gentle breeze, the soft swaying
of silken veils, a faint tinkling of tiny bells, a lover's
sigh, and the delicate perfume of desert flowers,
blooming somewhere in the blackness of the night.

II
EARTH, SEA, AND SKY

THE EAGLE

High above the towering pines,
Alive with morning light,
An eagle opened wide its wings,
And towards the sun took flight.

And as I stood beneath the trees,
And gazed up at the sky,
I felt my weight upon the earth,
But felt my spirit fly.

THE RIVER

The river echoed noisily
Between the mountain walls,
Then thundered down the mountainside
In tumbling waterfalls.
It rolled across the flattened land,
And toward a distant forest stand,
Then slipped between the silent trunks,
Through darkened tree-lined halls.
And then across a clearing bright,
The river ran all silver white,
Then crashed again down rock-filled slopes
And toward a distant shore,
Where from its narrow banks it sprang,
And fanned out wide and free,
Then raced across the foaming sand,
And mated with the sea.

THE THRASHER

He landed smartly on the lawn
And thought he'd idly pass
His time in search of millet seed
Hidden in the grass.

He did not see the crouching cat
Beneath the comfrey weed,
But thrust his bill among the blades
In search of hidden seed.

When suddenly, the comfrey weed
Exploded into black,
And cat's sharp claws encompassed him
And held him front and back.

The thrasher rose but inches high
In failed and futile flight,
He flicked his tail and flailed his wings,
A blur of brown and white.

Then back beneath the comfrey weed
Fled cat, and claws, and bird,
But of that silent murder there
No sound was ever heard.

And now upon the sun-filled lawn,
Among the millet seed,
A single feather lightly lies
Beside the bitter weed.

SPRING WAKES US

Spring wakes us with a gentleness —
    a light rain, the mysterious beginnings
    of buds and blossoms, the slow, subtle
    greening of the world, the unexpected
    appearance of a robin, the clearing of the sky.
Summer is less subtle and runs riot
    in green and yellow, with moist meadows,
    thick and alive with insects and flowers,
    and an intense heat from a sun that
    burns like molten gold in a vast
    expanse of blue.
Autumn finds summer exhausted and feverish,
    and cools her brow with sudden winds,
    gray skies, and cold rains; she turns
    down the sun and strips the gaudy greens
    from trees and fields, then colors the world
    in browns and grays.
Winter is cold, indifferent, and aloof,
    allowing bitter cold winds to carry
    along the snow and ice that envelop the
    world and bury all under a thick,
    muffling blanket of white.
And then, after a long cold stillness,
    Spring wakes us . . . .

AT THE LAKE

The lake lay calm
    against the shore,
The still, unbroken surface
    of the water reflecting
A bank of soft white clouds
    that hung unmoving
In the blue expanse
    of sky overhead.

Close to the water's edge
    stood a heavy stand
Of towering pines — dark green
    spires that pointed upward
Toward the sun, that hung
    fat and golden
Above the tranquil lake.

And, over all, an enveloping heat,
    rich with the smell
Of ripe green vegetation,
    and the subtle music
Of summer insects.

And then, suddenly,
    in random and erratic flight,
Two bright yellow butterflies.

MOUNTAINS

The mountains rest upon the earth
Like weary giants deep in thought,
And round their heads are ragged clouds
That on their jagged brows have caught.

And neath their cloaks of snow and ice
That round their shoulders fall,
They wait in stony silence
For the mountain gods to call.

And patiently they huddle there,
And patiently they wait,
For an eagle to come on silent wings
To reveal their ancient fate.

THUS MAY THE DARKNESS

The pavement was cracked
    by some insistent power,
Through which grew the seedling
    of a fragile flower.

Thus may the darkness
    of the darkest night
Be pierced by the power
    of the smallest light.

WIND

Sometimes still or barely moving,
Or, as gentle breezes, calm and cooling,
Or full of bluster, blowing free,
Or driving hard against the sea,
Full of salt and stinging spray,
And raging on in disarray,
Blowing wild with haunting moan,
An icy wind that chills the bone.

And then, when all the rage is spent,
The raging wind will then relent,
And then, as tranquil gentle breeze,
Will blow inland among the trees,
And dance among the dancing leaves,
And then, on lazy summer days,
Will sail along in gentler ways,
Dispelling heat and summer haze.

But then in some mysterious way,
On some uncertain future day,
It will again with whirling wrath,
Blast all that lies within its path.
Oh, wind, upon which clouds sail by,
Blow not with rage against the sky,
But let your whirling blowing cease,
And sail along in airy peace.

SPRING

Beneath the frozen landscape,
Without form and without sound,
Lies the hope that springs eternal
From the winter-hardened ground.
For when the ice is loosened
And begins to melt away,
Then the seed that long lay dormant
In a bed of hardened clay,
Will wake to seek the warming sun
And the golden light of day.
And though among the blackened boughs
A winter wind still sings,
Up through the bleak and barren ground
A slender seedling springs.

I LIKE A DAY

I like a day when it's cloudy and gray,
When the air has a bit of a chill,
When the wind blows free,
And there's only me,
At the top of a lonely hill,
And there's nothing to hear,
And there's nothing to see,
And there's only the wind, and me.

SUMMER NIGHTS

The music of a summer night
floats gently on the heated air,
as one by one the day's inhabitants
retreat to hideaways and sleep,
while those that are quickened
by the moon emerge to sing
their summer songs . . .
   the cricket's scratchy tune,
   the peeper's marshy melody,
   the bullfrog's deep-throated serenade,
   the cicada's high whining chorus,
   the needle-like bizzz of the mosquito,
   the dazzled moths tapping against
     porch lights and screens . . .
all floating gently into the summer night
on the warm and humid air.

SITTING UNDER AN APPLE TREE

Sitting under an apple tree,
Just taking in the sun,
I found how peace and happiness
Can come to anyone.

And that is . . .

Sitting under an apple tree,
Just taking in the sun.

YEAR ROUND

Spring is the season that awakens the Earth,
That restores and renews, a time of rebirth.

Summer is the season that was promised
    by Spring,
It is sunlight, green meadows, and birds
    on the wing.

Autumn is the season of quiet reflection,
A time for rethinking and deep introspection.

Winter is the season of ice and of snow,
When Earth is asleep and icicles grow.

But when the ice loosens and melts in the sun,
Then Earth will awaken, for Spring has begun.

BUT I DON'T KNOW WHY

The moon glows white,
The sun burns gold,
The jungle is hot,
The arctic is cold,
The ocean is wet,
The desert is dry,
I'm a part of it all,
But I don't know why.

HIDDEN LAKE

I came upon a sudden clearing,
A burst of blue amid the green,
While all about were darkened woods
That hid a lake I'd never seen.

And though I knew these woods quite well,
Had tramped old trails laid thick with moss,
There was no hint that there it lay,
A quarter mile across.

And as I stood at the water's edge,
And viewed this wondrous scene,
I felt I'd come upon a place
That none had ever seen.

And though the woods were close and dark,
The lake was bathed in light,
And the air was alive with the singing of birds,
Though there were no birds in sight.

The water was clear and silver blue,
The leaves were trembling on the trees,
And though the woods were hot and damp,
Here was a cooling breeze.

And the sky above was a summer blue,
White clouds floated lazily by,
And the air was filled with the
    sweetest perfume,
And I marveled as I looked at the sky.

And all around the water's edge
Grew flowers of every hue,
And though the woods were old and dark,
    with moss, and mold, and gloom,
The lake was fresh and new.

It was a glorious sight —
    a glorious and magical sight —
But just as it all had suddenly appeared,
The sky quickly darkened — the trees
    came together —
And the lake and the light disappeared.

And ever since then (sixty years or more),
I have searched for that magical scene,
That silver blue lake in the deepest woods,
That no one had ever seen.

But now I am old,
And I walk there with pain,
But still I must search,
Though I search there in vain.

For I long so to see
That blue lake and the sky,
That I'll tramp those old woods,
And I'll search till I die.

JAY

A voice like a rusty pump handle,
A bright blue and white suit, with
    an attitude to match,
No shy and contemplative bird is he,
Quick-darting, greedy, self-assured,
Indifferent to the social niceties,
Restless, jaunty, and with a feather
    in his cap,
And a voice like a rusty pump handle.

ROBIN

Pleasant, well mannered, neighborly,
With a good-sized appetite and a belly
    to match;
A conservative dresser, but with a
    fondness for red-orange vests;
A solid citizen — serious, sober, hard
    working, with strong family values;
Unassuming, undemanding, thoughtful,
    and perfectly content on the lawn.

ABOVE ME, THE SKY WAS EMPTY

I broke at last through a dense stand
    of tall trees and heavy underbrush and
    came upon a narrow clearing that
    bordered the jagged edge of a huge crag
    of raw stone, beyond which the mountain
    fell away into a deep canyon a mile
    or more below.

Above me, the sky was empty, except for
    the dark silhouette of a lone eagle, its
    wings outstretched and still, as it
    caught the rising currents of air and sailed
    slowly across the slate-gray sky.

As I stood there, at the very edge of the
    great stone crag, and looked out over the vast
    canyon below, I watched the silhouette of the
    eagle grow ever smaller until it disappeared
    and there was nothing but emptiness and silence,
    and then, after a long while, I made my way
    back to the trees, while behind me, out on the
    crag, the wind blew cold and steady
    into the canyon below.

INDIAN SUMMER

Winter's on its way . . .
    or is it?
Has summer come again
    to pay another visit?
But then I feel that autumn chill,
    and see that graying sky,
And know that summer's
    come again,
But just to say . . . good-bye.

THE SEASONS

Spring is a new-sprung seedling,
Summer is a bird flying free,
Autumn is a frozen cornfield,
And winter's a leafless tree.

Spring is full of promise,
Summer is joyful and free,
Autumn's a time for reflection,
And winter's a leafless tree.

LATE AUTUMN

Slate-gray skies,
A small white sun, shining dimly
    through ragged windswept clouds,
    casting a gray half-light and little heat,
Wisps of distant smoke from farmhouse
    chimneys and mounds of burning leaves,
Dark brown fields with endless rows
    of dry yellow stubble,
The scratchy, scattering dance of yellow-
    orange leaves across the gray-black
    asphalt of country roads,
A solitary bird — small, brown, and
    motionless — huddled on a length
    of rusted wire,
And in the air, a cold wet wind that
    whispers of colder, harsher days
    to come, when the hard frozen edge
    of winter will cut like a knife
    through wool, through flannel,
    to the bone.

BUT NOW IT MAKES NO SENSE

It was a summer Sunday afternoon,
And I was resting in the sun,
Just resting 'cause it felt so good,
And all my chores were done.

It was all so jolly peaceful,
And life seemed so serene,
The apple trees were all in bloom,
And the fields were lush and green.

The sky was an optimistic blue,
There wasn't a cloud in the sky,
And all the world was right and just,
And I didn't question why.

The entire world — and life itself —
Seemed to make such sense,
That to question it seemed foolish,
And more than a little dense.

But a sudden, burning, searing pain
Changed my rosy view,
For a bumblebee had stung me,
As bees are wont to do.

And now I sit with ice on ear,
Until the pain relents,
A moment ago, life was just,
But now it makes no sense!

SING A SONG

Sing a song of acid rain
From out a leaden sky,
Man has walked upon the moon
But cannot reason why
The Earth is filled with fear and hate
And whales have learned to cry.

Sing a song of acid rain,
Of leaves the trees are bare,
No birds do fly, no birds do sing,
Upon the bitter air,
And on the Earth, there's little left
Of all that once was fair.

Sing a song of acid rain,
There's fire in the sky,
Man is in the counting house
Counting reasons why
The oil must flow, and profits grow,
While Earth is left to die.

Sing a song of acid rain,
Of leaves the trees are bare,
No birds do fly, no birds do sing,
Upon the bitter air,
And on the Earth, there's little left
Of all that once was fair.

PROFIT IS THE BENEDICTION

Scrape the earth down to the quick,
Cut away the trees and grass,
Peel away the earthen flesh,
Reveal an anthracitic mass.

Take the coal and leave the scar,
An open wound for wind and rain,
Let the earthen flesh decay,
There's profit in this earthen pain.

Continue on, there's more to find,
Copper, phosphates, iron ore,
Tear away the earthen flesh,
Extend for miles the open sore.

Continue on, there's more to find,
Continue on, there's no restriction,
Riches lie beneath the soil,
Profit is the benediction!

THE EARTH WE DESPOIL

We clear-cut the forests,
We foul the sweet air,
We dump in the oceans,
We destroy what is there.
We strip-mine the coal,
We pump out the oil,
We seek the Earth's riches,
The Earth we despoil.

MIDWINTER'S EVE

Black sky,
White moon,
Clear,
Silent,
Brittle with cold.

Darkness
Everywhere,
Except
For
Moonlight
On a
Small cloud
Of
Frozen
Breath.

A SOLITARY BIRD

A solitary bird,
small, brown, and cold,
on a wire fence,
rusted, broken, and old.

IN THE MIDDLE OF THE NIGHT

Tell me, dear, what did you hear
In the middle of the night,
That woke you up with such a start
And gave you such a fright?

Did you hear the great horned owl
Calling in the night,
Or was it just the restless wind
That gave you such a fright?

Or did you hear a distant train
And hear its mournful tune,
Or did you hear a lonely wolf
Baying at the moon?

Oh, tell me, dear, what did you hear
In the middle of the night,
That woke you up with such a start
And gave you such a fright?

Did you hear the distant thunder
Rumbling in the night,
Or was it just a barking dog
That gave you such a fright?

Did you hear a cricket sing
Beneath the moon's pale light,
Or was it just a dazzled moth
Tapping at the light?

Or did you hear the old oak clock
Ticking in the hall,
Or was it just a tiny mouse
Scratching in the wall?

Oh, tell me, dear, what did you hear
In the middle of the night,
That woke you up with such a start
And gave you such a fright?

Oh, do not fear the sounds you hear
In the middle of the night,
Just close your eyes and go to sleep
And I will hold you tight.

So, hush, my dear, and do not fear
The sounds you hear at night,
Just close your eyes and go to sleep
And I will hold you tight.

IN THE WOODS

I thought I saw a woodland elf
    upon a mushroom stool,
But when I went to tell the world,
    they said I was a fool,
So now I never tell a soul,
    for fear that they were right.
Still, the thought of what
    I thought I saw
Fills me with delight.

THE FLOWERS OF OUR DREAMING

The flowers of our dreaming
Bloom in colors rarely seen,
Not the colors of the rainbow,
But the colors in between.

But those flowers cannot blossom
In the sun-bright light of noon,
But only in dark places,
In the pale light of the moon.

And in the dark the moonlight glows,
And casts its magic light,
That grows the flowers of our dreams,
While we dream away the night.

But even as they bloom they fade,
Though we water them with tears,
Each lovely flower blooms but once,
Then forever disappears.

Oh, the flowers of our dreaming,
They blossom all unseen,
In a place we cannot visit
Till we go there in a dream.

Yes, the flowers of our dreaming
Are flowers you won't find,
For they're planted in our dreams,
And bloom only in our mind.

I WATCHED THE HAWK

I watched the hawk,
Its wings outstretched and stiff,
The feathers at the tips curving upward,
Sensitive to the rising currents of air
As it circled slowly, like a dream,
Above the dark green spires of ponderosa pine
That towered above me.

I stood and watched,
Conscious of my weight upon the earth,
Until the dark silhouette of the bird
Disappeared into a mist of mountain fog
And low-hanging clouds.
And then, when the sky was empty,
I looked down at the earth,
Laid thick with moss,
And slowly, wearily, moved on.

WHODUNIT

I found some feathers
   from a dove
Lying by the walk,
   while up above,
Looking quite content,
   a handsome red-tailed hawk.

REGATTA

Windswept waves fall and rise,
Swelling sails take shape and size,
The narrow hulls reflect the sun,
They pass the buoys one by one
And knife the water clean in two,
Sky and water, blue on blue,
The streaming bows plunge and rise,
The soaring gulls cry startled cries,
The ocean roars and sighs and sings,
The salt sea foams, the ship's bell rings,
The mast and rigging, deck and sail,
Creak and groan an ancient tale
Of wind and water, ships and sea,
Of sun and sky, of rum and tea,
Wind and water, gulls and sail,
Crashing waves and Ahab's whale,
It's all the legend of the sea,
Before the wind, and sailing free!

THE FLYING FISH

From the green-black depths of the ocean,
He swims up toward the sky,
And from his watery world he springs
With fins outstretched to fly.

Poor fish, he cannot be content
To fly beneath the sea,
But longs to join the soaring gulls,
Forever flying free!

OH, WHAT A VARIED PLACE IS EARTH

Oh, what a varied place is Earth,
From winter's death to spring's rebirth,
From the hard white world of arctic ice
To a dreamy island paradise,
From mountain peaks that pierce the sky
To golden plains of wheat and rye,
From rolling hills of forest trees
To rivers, lakes, and inland seas,
From steaming jungles and tropic lands
To trackless wastes of desert sands,
From teeming cities of man and motion
To the endless expanse of sky and ocean,
From the perfumed heart of a fragile flower
To the eye of a hurricane's awesome power,
Oh, what a varied place is Earth,
From winter's death to spring's rebirth.

JAGUAR

The jaguar moves with liquid ease
Through tangled vines and jungle trees,
Through green-black shadows and sunlit gold,
In jungles wet and dark and old,
That smell of heat and mold and death,
That smell of blood and jaguar's breath,
And then his golden form is still,
His claws extended for the kill,
And there in hiding he will stay,
His head is lowered, and now he'll prey.

AND, ONCE AGAIN . . .

A sky full of stars
That glitter and shine,
A pale moon rises
Over towering pine.

The night sky glitters
Above the lake,
The woods are deep,
The peepers wake.

The moon is full,
A lone wolf cries,
The owl hunts,
A field mouse dies.

The sky grows pink,
Then gold and blue,
The sun bursts forth,
The day is new.

The day wears on,
The clouds drift by,
The sun sinks low
In a graying sky.

The sun has set,
The night is clear,
And, once again,
The stars appear.

LITTLE THINGS

Spring comes in little things . . .
In the small incremental quickenings
    of life — the unexpected appearance of
    an ant, a small spider, a housefly,
In the softening of the ice on the lake and
    the sudden falling of icicles from the eaves,
In the gradual shifting of the wind from the
    north to the west,
In the subtle greening of the lawn,
In the long, trailing Vs of geese pointing north,
In the small yellow-green buds swelling
    at the tips of the tiniest branches,
In the sudden and unexpected appearance
    of a robin on the still frozen lawn,
In the gradual bluing of the sky after
    endless days of slate gray, and the
    forming of large white fleecy clouds,
In the leafing of trees and shrubs, and the
    unexpected appearance of the first crocus,
And, finally, in the sudden bursting forth
    of the sun.

EVERY SO OFTEN

The old man was bent and weary,
   with little hope;
The earth was hard and dry,
   with little promise;
The seed was old and cracked,
   with little life;
The sky was gray and overcast,
   with little sun;
The wind was strong and steady,
   with cutting cold.

Months later, the corn was high,
   and ripe, and sweet.

Moral:
Every so often,
   without rhyme or reason,
Life surprises,
   and has its season.

III
PAST, PRESENT, FUTURE

APARTMENT 5B

A yellow flower on the windowsill,
It flowered there and always will.
Though years have passed, I still recall
That yellow flower, so straight and tall.
A gentle scene of vase and flower
Against the city's awful power,
Against the noise, the soot, the grime,
Against the traffic and the crime,
Against the steel, the brick, the wall,
That yellow flower, so straight and tall.
Oh, I remember, and always will,
That yellow flower on the windowsill.

CHOICES

Yesterday,
While the city slept,
Two men used
Razor-sharp blades
To cut the living flesh
Of a young woman.

One used a knife
To end her life;
The other, a scalpel,
To save it.

THE CITY
Night

A kaleidoscope of flashing lights
    and stone-filled shadows,
Of wet asphalt, plumes of white steam,
    and empty buses,
Of black and white police cars
    and glossy yellow taxis,
Of dance halls, movie houses, bars,
    and blue and orange neon,
Of dimly lit hallways, crying babies,
    and windowshades,
Of distant sirens, sudden shouts,
    and broken glass,
Of rats, and mice, and roaches,
Of empty streets, dark alleyways,
    and cats,
Of sighs, and moans, and quiet sobbing.
And everywhere, a million sleeping bodies,
    curled in fetal fear,
While in the darkened streets
    someone is running,
    someone is coughing,
    someone is dying.

Day

A symphony of shouts and curses,
Of heavy trucks, and buses,
    and quick darting taxis,
Of brick, and glass, and steel,
Of flags, awnings, and umbrellas,
Of sudden bursts of color and sound,
Of sunlight and gray drizzle,
Of steam, squealing brakes, and horns,
Of broad boulevards, sidewalk cafes,
    and cobblestone streets,
Of apartment buildings, pushcarts,
    and crying babies,
Of asphalt, concrete, and garbage,
Of barking dogs, sudden shouts,
    and the shrill scream of sirens and whistles.
And everywhere, the smell
    of garlic, burnt rubber, and gasoline.
And everywhere, the alternating rush
    of automobiles and people . . .
    of automobiles and people . . .
    of automobiles and people . . .

UPON THIS FIELD

Here I stand, upon this field,
In kingly isolation,
While all about, both fore and back,
Is naught but desolation.

And my fair queen, who at my side,
Stood in silent expectation,
Now lies beneath this checkered field,
Beyond all consolation.

And my twin castles, once strong and proud,
Prevented not their penetration
By a fearless foe, who captured both,
With shouts of exultation.

And those good bishops, though they prayed
With holy incantation,
Were able not to save their souls,
Nor prevent annihilation.

And those brave knights, whose hearts were filled
With wild anticipation,
Now sing no more the joys of war
In youthful celebration.

And all my men, mere pawns of fate,
Who fought with desperation,
Fell to the ground with shouts of hate
And cries of lamentation.

And so upon this field I stand,
And here await my fate,
A final blow, from a ruthless foe,
And his awful cry of . . ."Mate!"

WHAT MAN HAS DONE TO MAN

There is no evil in the world,
Since the course of time began,
That's caused as many tears to fall
As the evil done by man.

No, there is no evil in the world,
Since the course of time began,
That can match the awful horror of
What man has done to man.

HAVING ENEMIES

Having enemies is
    a common curse,
But one false friend
    is even worse!

JOE'S BAR

There are no clocks in Joe's bar,
   and if there are, they're hard
To read in the smokey haze
   of cigarette and cigar.

A smokey haze that's illuminated
   by the dull glow of colored lights,
Blue and orange neon and small table
   lamps that turn days into nights.

The air is fetid and rank in Joe's bar,
   it's been breathed many times before,
A sour air that carries with it the smell
   of stale beer and vomit on the floor.

There are no dreams in Joe's bar,
   and if there are, they're hard to find,
The dreamers swallowed them long ago
   and can't remember where they are.

There is no joy in Joe's bar, where
   crying sounds like laughter,
And hope is dead for the here and now,
   and the here and hereafter.

They're changing the name of Joe's bar
   for a name that cuts like a knife;
Joe wants a more descriptive name,
   He's calling it, "That's Life!"

TO BE THOROUGHLY FIT

A muscle,
To be thoroughly fit,
Must be disciplined
And worked hard
Each day of its life.
And it must be nourished,
Both by the bright blood of passion
And the clear oxygen of reason,
Yet it must not become
    bound, rigid, or unyielding,
But must remain flexible
    and responsive.

The heart is a muscle.

LIFE

Living life by inches
    is not living life at all,
It's like falling in love with someone
    while trying to avoid the fall.

No, the only way to live a life
    is to hold nothing back at all,
To put your life where your heart is,
    then simply risk it all!

MUSIC

Listen to . . .

the sweet, sad, mournful melancholy
and warm chocolate syrup longing
of the cello,

the bright brassy urgency and lemon-
drop sweetness of the trumpet,

the quick-darting, high-flying, flag-waving
teapot eccentricity of the flute,

the grand explosiveness and wild heart-
pounding thumping of the bass drum
and timpani,

the thick, rich, cream-in-your-coffee mellowness
and sweet taffy-pull sensuousness of the
slide trombone,

the airy waterfalling melodiousness, dreamy
romanticism, and bubbling champagne of
the harp,

the high, thin, soul-stirring intensity and sweet
poignancy of the violin,

the serious, sober, well-mannered, intelligent,
and disciplined voice of the viola,

the sweet black licorice and low-down,
jive-jumping, good-news wailing of
the clarinet,

the haunting, high-in-the-Alps, and
Black Forest mysticism of the French
horn,

the always reliable, easy-going, and
down-in-your-shoes rhythms of the
string bass,

the frenetic, hyperactive, rapid-fire frenzy,
and gotta-go-to-war syncopation of the
snare drum,

the high-spirited, helium-inhaling
falsetto, and whistling lunacy of the
piccolo,

the thick, warm blackstrap molasses
and deep-in-your-belly growl of the
bassoon,

the high, nasal, hypnotic whine and
belly-dance, snake-in-a-basket
melodies of the oboe,

the uninhibited, in-your-face heroics
and melodramatic explosiveness of
the cymbal,

the down-and-out, gut-wrenching grittiness,
and after-hours melancholy of the
saxophone,

the rag-time, boogie-woogie, be-bopping jazziness,
and glorious melt-your-heart romanticism, and
black and white sophistication of the piano,

the thunderous power and hallelujah glory
of the pipe organ,

the slightly tipsy, happy-go-lucky, and
schizophrenic eccentricity of the triangle,

the muscular tugboat toughness of the tuba,

And finally . . .

there's a man in a black and white tux,
with a stick, and when he's got it all together,
you can hear the foot-stomping, heart-
throbbing, tear-jerking, toe-tapping,
hand-clapping, finger-snapping, mind-
blowing, awe-inspiring, and soul-
stirring sounds of Life itself!

MADAM SOPHIA

Madam Sophia could foretell the future,
And nothing from her could hide,
And love and joy were in her future,
For the cards had never lied.

Yes, Madam Sophia could foretell the future,
"It's a gift," she often cried,
"And love and joy are in my future,
For the cards have never lied."

Oh, Madam Sophia could foretell the future,
And she saw herself as a bride,
And love and joy awaited her,
For the cards had never lied.

Yes, Madam Sophia could foretell the future,
And with joy she laughed and cried,
For love and joy were in the cards,
And the cards had never lied.

Oh, Madam Sophia had foretold the future,
And she waited with joy and pride,
And she waited and waited until she was old,
For the cards had never lied.

Poor Madam Sophia had foretold the future,
But she never became a bride,
And there she sat with the cards in her hand,
And there she sat . . . and died.

AUDREY ROSE

She ran away from her parents' farm,
A thousand miles away,
To see the city, and the lights,
Where all was bright and gay.

And there she met a handsome man,
Whose smile lit up the night,
She gave her heart and soul to him,
And soon he held her tight.

And on the streets he made her walk,
Where he sold her for a fee,
And night and day he sold her soul,
And would not let her free.

And one by one, they held her tight,
With urgent loving hate,
And crushed the laughing girl within,
And Death could hardly wait.

And now her lifeless body lies
Upon a bed of stone,
Her youthful form beneath a sheet,
She lies there all alone.

Oh, yesterday, she whirled about,
And laughed at life and men,
And now she lies there all alone,
Where she'll never laugh again.

And back among the greening hills,
Upon the little farm,
Her parents wonder how she fared,
And if she came to harm.

And her mother prays she'll find her girl,
Though she knows not where or when,
But fears that she will never see
Her Audrey Rose again.

A SUBTLE MAGIC

Your presence works a subtle magic,
Like sudden sunlight through parting clouds,
Or a burst of yellow butterflies across
   a darkened meadow,
Or the wind through groves of aspen trees
That shakes the green and silvered leaves,
Then weaves through fields of golden wheat,
A cooling breeze against the heat,
Or sudden bursts of morning light
That pierce the darkness of the night
And fill the sky with pink and gold,
The Earth in sunlight to enfold,
And when in my embrace you're curled,
I find your kiss can change the world.

THE DRUNKARD'S TALE

Upon a tray of silver and gold
This crystal vessel stands,
And on the silver and on the gold
Reflect the crimson strands
Of that hell, that bloody hell,
That no one understands.

What is it in this crystal vessel
That holds me in its sway?
What is it in this bloody hell
That commands my brain to stay,
And drink and drink to quench this thirst
That eats my soul away?

And when I've drunk and gaze therein
And see a life like mine,
I fill the vessel to the brim
To see a life divine,
But only when the glass is full
Can I see it in the wine.

ARE YOU GETTING ANYWHERE?

You're striving for success
And it looks like you'll succeed,
But is there joy and happiness
In accomplishing the deed?

If you fail to smell the flowers
Or in joy you fail to share,
Then ask yourself the question,
"Am I getting anywhere?"

And while it all depends
On how you use the term,
In striving for success alone,
There's a lesson you will learn.

If you fail to smell the flowers
Or in joy you fail to share,
Then even if you do succeed,
You've not gotten anywhere.

For in the end, when you're all alone,
And there's no one with whom to share,
Then you'll wish you had asked
    the question,
"Am I getting anywhere?"

So stop to smell the flowers
And in joy be sure to share,
For then you'll know for certain
If you've gotten anywhere.

ON FIRST LOOKING INTO
*HAWLEY'S CHEMICAL DICTIONARY**

Who says that scientists
Have no heart or passion,
That they do not wish upon the stars,
But only count them,
That they do not hear the music
   of the spheres
And worship only reason,
That they do not love, or fear, or hate?

On opening *Hawley's Chemical Dictionary*,
I found the entry, "POEMS,"
Clear evidence that the Humanities
Are alive and well, even in the laboratory,
And that while beauty and passion
Cannot be measured or analyzed,
They are experienced and valued, even there.

But, alas, I found too late
It was not poetry that was intended,
No verses here on life, or love,
   or man's inexorable fate,
But only a simple acronym for . . .
Poly-oxy-ethylene-mono-stearate.

Hawley's Condensed Chemical Dictionary, 11th ed., page 930.

LISTEN

Listen to the nations,
    They are vying;
Listen to the leaders,
    They are lying;
Listen to the bombers,
    They are flying;
Listen to the children,
    They are crying;
Listen to the Earth,
    It is dying.

FANATICS

They know what they know,
And believe what they know,
And that's the short and the long,
'Cause fanatics can believe
    most anything,
Except that they are wrong!

HISTORY

"Tell me, Master, what hast thou
learned from reading history?"

"I've learned, my son, that men
are fools, and the rest is a mystery."

BLOW THE BUGLE

Blow the bugle loud and clear,
Bang the rhythmic drum,
See the soldiers marching,
    marching,
Each one with a gun.

See their shiny buttons gleaming,
Hear their weapons rattle,
See the soldiers marching,
    marching,
Off they go to battle.

Hear the cheering and the shouts,
Hear the church bells ringing,
See the soldiers marching,
    marching,
Hear the crowds all singing.

See their bright new uniforms,
The banners waving high,
See the soldiers marching,
    marching,
Hear their mothers cry.

GLORY IS FOR THE LIVING

Glory is for the living,
For it's we who sound the drum,
It's we who sing the anthem
For the deeds the dead have done.

It's the living who obey the call,
Who march to drum and fife,
Who sing of country, right or wrong,
Then sharpen sword and knife.

Glory is for the living,
For when a soldier dies,
He lies unthinking in the grave,
He knows not truth nor lies.

For it's only when he's living
That glory is the prize,
But when the sword cuts to the bone
That's when the glory dies.

Yes, glory is for the living,
For the dead can die but once,
And it's here among the living
That Death for glory hunts.

THE BATTLE FLAGS WERE RAISED ON HIGH

The battle flags were raised on high,
Green and gold against the sky,
The drummer drummed a marching tune,
To which they marched from dawn till noon,
Their uniforms were crisp and clean,
They swelled with pride when they were seen.

Five hundred horses, a thousand men,
They marched along in rows of ten,
Until they came upon a field,
On which they knew their fate was sealed,
For in the distance they could spy
A hundred battle flags raised on high.

They fluttered in the autumn breeze,
Red and black against the trees,
A hundred banners raised on high,
To which they sang their battle cry,
And when they finished that fighting song,
They stood and waited — ten thousand strong!

While across the field, with banners high,
They knew that day they'd come to die,
And there they stood in silent dread,
And there a thousand prayers were said,
But still they stood where they were led
To fight against the black and red.

Then all was silent except the breeze
That shook the dry and dying leaves,
The horses stamped and pawed the ground,
Their nostrils flared, their eyes were round,
They moved their weight from side to side,
Their muscles quivered beneath their hide.

And then across the open sky,
A single blackbird circled high,
The wind increased and it was cold,
It whipped the flags of green and gold,
And then it swirled and faster sped,
Then blew against the black and red.

Then in the sky another bird,
A second blackbird, then a third,
And soon across the darkening sky,
A hundred blackbirds circled high,
The wind blew hard and wet and cold
Against the black and red, the green and gold.

Then, suddenly, a trumpet call,
That froze the blood of one and all,
And for a moment, no one stirred,
But then a second call was heard,
And when they heard that second sound,
They charged across the open ground.

Across the field, through shot and shell,
The horses charged into that hell,
The riders held their sabers high,
And cried their awful battle cry,
And then the men, ten thousand strong,
Into the battle charged headlong.

The cannons roared a thunderous sound,
Throwing men and horses to the ground,
Shrapnel and bullets filled the air,
And death and terror were everywhere,
The shells came whistling a piercing sound,
And exploded on the blood-soaked ground.

Onward they charged, in blood they were mired,
Sabers were flashed, guns were fired,
The cannons still roared with tongues of flame,
While bullets were playing a deadly game,
The field was aflame, the sky was aglow,
A flag bearer fell and was killed with a blow.

The air was filled with fire and smoke,
They could not breathe but cough and choke,
They could not run but stumble and fall,
The smoke was black and covered all,
And through the flames they tried to flee,
But through the smoke they could not see.

And then there was one final charge
Against the enemy's deadly barrage,
The cannons' roar was a deafening sound,
That split the air and shook the ground,
And a thousand more lay in Death's embrace,
And surprise and horror were on his face.

Then all was quiet on the field of blood,
The dead and dying lay in the mud,
And over all, the sky was red,
As was the field where they had bled,
The dead and dying, ten thousand strong,
It was hard to tell who was right or wrong.

Now all was quiet, there was no sound,
Now all was still on the blood-soaked ground,
And there on the field, among the dead,
Lay flags and banners of black and red,
And in their arms, now still and cold,
There lay the flags of green and gold.

I WONDER

I wonder if the dead can hear
The shouts of victory,
The banging drum, the bugle's call,
And all the revelry.

And do they hear the endless tales
Of the glory of their deed,
Of how they charged through shot
   and shell,
To which they paid no heed.

Of how they fought and nobly died
For honor and for glory,
And do they hear the children beg
To hear again the story.

Oh, I do not think the dead can hear
How we the living lie,
But if they could, I wonder would
They laugh, or would they cry.

THERE WAS A TAPPING AT MY WINDOW

There was a tapping at my window
   one dark and starless night,
But what it was I could not tell
   and held my breath in fright.

At first I could not clearly see
   what it was that I had heard,
But then out on the windowsill
   there appeared the strangest bird.

The feathers of its feathered coat
   lay smooth and flat and tight,
And shone like glossy satin shines
   and was blacker than the night.

And there it strutted back and forth
   along the windowsill,
Stopping now and then to strike the glass
   with a large and pointed bill.

And then it fixed me with a rounded eye
   that shone like molten gold,
Then cocked its head, and then it said,
   "Let me in. The wind is bitter cold."

But I would not open the window,
   'What bird is this?' I wondered.
"Let me in and I'll grant your every wish," it
   said, then lightning flashed and it thundered.

But I could not move and froze with fear,
   I could not — would not — let it in,
And again it struck against the glass
   with a bill as black as sin.

"This is your final chance," it warned,
   "I have diamonds and gold to share.
Let me in! Let me in!" it screeched again,
   but again I would not dare.

And so, in fear, I kept it out,
   and with a look of anger and pity,
It opened wide its great black wings
   and flew up and over the city.

And as I watched it fly away,
   its wings rising and falling,
I felt a terrible sadness,
   and I thought I heard it calling.

"You made your choice and it is final,
   and I will call on you no more,
And you will live in your narrow world,
   where you'll live forevermore."

And again I felt a great sadness.
  Had paradise been so near?
Oh, why did I not let it enter?
  Was it only out of fear?

And now, each night, I wait by the window
  and wonder if I was right.
Should I have listened to that magical bird?
  Should I have let it in that night?

———

THERE IS A ROAD

There is a road that has no end,
There always is another bend,
And round that bend another turn,
With something new to see and learn,
And though I've traveled for many a mile,
I'd like to travel on a while,
For there's a restlessness in me
That fills me with a need to see
What lies beyond that further bend
And if the road comes to an end,
And though I'm weary and long to rest,
I'll put my spirit to the test
And travel round that further bend,
And travel on until the end.

———

LOST AND ALONE

There is no loneliness that cuts quite
    so deep as standing lost and alone
    in the middle of a large and crowded
    city, surrounded by the loud and
    dissonant symphony of city sounds,
    by broad boulevards and narrow
    cobblestone streets that wind maze-
    like between rows of towering
    buildings — huge sky-scraping blocks
    of stone, steel, and glass — by an endless
    roaring parade of quick-darting
    automobiles and the heavy rumbling
    of trucks and buses, and by great
    hordes of people, all rushing by
    with an intense and hurried urgency,
    fearful of being late for their
    individual appointments with
    life . . . and death.

And I stand there — lost and alone —
    ignored by the passing crowd —
    unseen and unheard by everyone
    but myself.

IV
NIGHTFALL

OFTEN, AT NIGHTFALL

Often, at nightfall, when the last glowing
   remnant of twilight fades away and
   the sun sinks slowly and wearily into
   the darkness, I am overwhelmed with
   a great sadness.

And while the evening sky is often filled
   with countless points of light and by
   the pale gleaming of the moon, there is
   a silence — a stillness — that overtakes
   the soul and whispers of loneliness and loss.

But then I feel your presence, and your touch,
   and I am comforted, and I curl into your
   warm and protective embrace, and I feel
   your breath upon my cheek, and I hear you
   whisper my name, and I am consumed by love.

But even as I feel the beating of your heart
   against my chest, and feel your warmth
   enfolding me, and hear you speak my name,
   I see in the fading twilight, in the setting sun,
   the coming of a night that is without
   light, without warmth, without love,
   without end.

THEY SAT ALONE
An Old Man

He sat alone on a wooden bench
In a park across the way,
And watched the sky turn gray again
At the end of another day.

And as he sat, alone and still,
The day turned into night,
And shadows soon encircled him
Beneath the moon's pale light.

And in the dark, and in his mind,
Were the voices of his youth,
His father's, stern, and filled with facts,
His mother's, filled with truth.

And he heard the quiet sobbing
Of a sweetheart long ago,
Who held him in her arms one night
And begged him not to go.

But he was young and full of dreams,
And so he left her side,
But promised to return one day
And claim her as his bride.

But sixty years had come and gone
Since he was in his youth,
And there were dreams and hopes
    and schemes,
But very little truth.

And so he sat alone each day
In the park across the way,
And wondered where the years had gone,
And how he'd lost his way.

But the sand was falling in the glass
As darkness filled the sky,
And the voices dimmed,
And the faces blurred,
And a cold wet wind blew by.

And then the sun came up again
And children came to play,
But the old man sat alone and still,
Till they found he'd passed away.

And now the old man sits no more
In the park across the way,
And near the bench the pigeons strut,
And children laugh and play.

And now the old man sits no more
In the park across the way,
Where lovers sit and whisper lies,
And the days all pass away . . .

And the days all pass away.

An Old Woman

She sat alone on a wooden chair
In a room across the hall,
And watched the fading sunlight
Reflected on the wall.

And there she sat, alone and still,
Until the day was gone,
And moonlight filled the silent room
As night came slowly on.

And in the moonlight on the wall
She saw the faces of her youth,
They had whispered he would break her
    heart,
But she would not hear the truth.

And she heard his youthful laughter,
As she heard it long ago,
When she held him in her arms one night,
And begged him not to go.

But he was young and full of dreams,
And so he left her side,
But promised to return one day
And claim her as his bride.

But sixty years had come and gone
Since he said that last good-bye,
And there were tears and hopes and fears,
But his promise was a lie.

And so she sat alone each day
At the Sunshine Nursing Home,
And wondered where the years had gone,
And why she was alone.

But then the moonlight faded,
And darkness covered all,
And the faces of her youth were gone,
And she heard the clock on the wall.

And then the sun came up again
At the dawn of another day,
And there she sat, alone and still,
Till they found she'd passed away.

And now she sits alone no more
In the room across the hall,
Where the sunlight filtered dimly in,
And no one came to call.

And now she sits alone no more
In the Home across the way,
Where all her silent tears were shed,
And the days all passed away . . .

And the days all passed away.

WHAT SHALL I SAY?

What shall I say this winter's day?
That winter's gloom will fade away,
That spring will come again someday,
That in the meadow and on the hill
Will bloom the golden daffodil,
That ice will melt and rivers flow,
And in the fields the crops will grow,
That in the blue and cloudless sky
The sun will warm and birds will fly,
And in their nests the birds will sing,
And love and hope will come with spring.
Is that what I should say,
This cold and lonely day?
Alas, the ice is holding fast,
For here's a winter that will not pass,
The sand has fallen in the glass.

ON THE WINDSWEPT PRAIRIE

On the windswept prairie,
on a wire fence,
Rests a small brown bird.

Winter has come,
the prairie is white,
And only the wind is heard.

WINTER

Winter is in the sky,
in the air,
in my bones.

Not a winter
of clean, white snow
and bright cold air
that invigorates the soul
and quickens the blood,
that reddens your cheeks,
your ears, and the tip
of your nose,
that repaints the world —
the roads, the fields,
the trees, the rooftops —
with a thick, fresh coat of white.

Not a winter
of laughter,
of seeing your breath,
of making angels in the snow,
of shoveling the walkway,
of stamping your booted feet
on the flagstone entryway
to get the snow off and to
bring back some feeling
into frozen toes,
of hot soup, runny noses,
and a crackling fire.

No, the winter
in my bones is a winter
of half-light — dull, gray,
and wet — and a bitter bone-
chilling wind that howls
through the cracks around
ill-fitting doors and windows —
a wind that moans, and sighs,
and sobs, like the cry of a
lost soul.

No, the winter
in my bones is not
of snow, but of ice —
a winter that day after day,
week after week, month
after unchanging month,
whispers in your ear that
you are weak, fragile,
vulnerable, and alone —
and cold — always cold.

No, the winter
in my bones is not
of a roaring fire that warms
the heart, but of little light,
and little heat,

of loneliness and regrets,
of leafless trees, and frozen earth,
and everywhere you look,
you see gray, dark gray, and black —
and always, there is the cold.

And then, once again,
I close my eyes and remember,
and see her, in a winter of our youth,
as she comes into the house with a
sudden rush of cold winter wind
and a swirl of snowflakes that cling
to her hair, and the wind catches the door
and it slams shut, and she is
startled, and we laugh, and she
speaks my name, and, in that moment,
winter is transformed into a season
of laughter, of joy, and of love.

But then, her presence fades, and
a darker, colder winter is
in the sky,
in the air,
in my bones.

AND DREAM THAT I AM THERE

The river flows serenely
As it makes its way along,
The sky above is cloudless
And the air is filled with song.

The meadow's full and whispering
In the sweet and gentle breeze,
And the flowers are all blooming
And the birds are in the trees.

The sun is warm and golden
And it shines upon your hair,
And I hear your silver laughter
And I dream that I am there.

But now the warming sun has set
And the air is damp and cold,
And though I dream that I am young
I know that I am old.

And so I dream of yesteryear
And of your golden hair,
And through my tears I see it all
And dream that I am there.

OH, WHEN DID I GROW OLD?

The sky is overcast and gray,
The wind is wet and cold,
Winter's come, and come to stay,
Oh, when did I grow old?

The sun no longer shines as bright,
A grayness fills the sky,
The light is fading into night,
The days fly swiftly by.

The snow is falling, all is white,
I lean upon my cane,
I see ahead an endless night,
Each step is filled with pain.

The sky is overcast and gray,
The wind is wet and cold,
Winter's come, and come to stay,
Oh, when did I grow old?

HARRIET GREEN

Harriet Green was just seventeen
When they made her the Queen of the Fair,
The prettiest girl in Fulton County,
And they made her the Queen of the Fair.
But that was back in '32,
When she was young and all was new,
And Harriet Green was the prettiest of girls,
With the prettiest eyes, and the prettiest curls
That shone in the sun like gold.

But that was sixty years ago,
And now her hair is white as snow,
And she is under county care,
At a home not far from the County Fair,
Where she lives all alone in a nursing home,
Not far from the County Fair.

And there she sits in a tiny room,
From early morning to evening's gloom,
With nothing to do but sit and stare,
And there's no one to talk to and no one to care,
And her only company is a radio,
Which she likes to hold in her lap.

Now Harriet Green, who was County Fair Queen,
More than half a century ago, sits all alone
In a nursing home, and listens to the radio,
That reports all the sports, and reports all the news,
That tells her the weather, and how to clean leather,
And exactly which products to use.

And the announcer sells cars, and there's news about Mars,
And the music is all rock-and-roll;
And there's news about crashes, and forests in ashes,
And the weather is sunny and fair;
And the shuttle has landed, the debt has expanded,
And there's murder in Tiananmen Square;
And the religion show host, who is louder than most,
Tells his listeners to pray and call in,
And he shouts about giving, and he shouts about sin,
And he shouts that you've got to call in.

And then there was news about jogging and shoes,
And news about money and sports,
And how to cash in on the latest in fashion,
And how to be free of warts.

And then the music began, about a woman's love for a man,
And when it was over, a commercial about "Rover,"
A dog food that comes in a can.

And then the show's host, who spoke faster than most,
Said, "Stay tuned for the news at seven!"
But Harriet Green, who was County Fair Queen,
Couldn't wait for the news at seven,
For her old lady's heart had stopped with a start,
And her old lady's soul was in heaven.

WHEN THE WORLD WAS SIX YEARS OLD

I remember we played in the snow all day,
And your nose was pink with cold,
And your laughter was like the ringing of bells,
And the world was six years old.

And I see you in summer with your hair flying free,
And it shone in the sun like gold,
And we ate green apples and I got sick,
And the world was six years old.

Oh, love, though now our hair is white,
And we huddle against the cold,
When I look at you and see your smile,
The world is six years old.

But since we know we soon must part,
There's something that needs to be told,
I love you now as I loved you then,
When the world was six years old.

YESTERDAY

Yesterday,
In a crowded room,
A young girl I did see,
Whose eyes and lips
Did speak of love,
Though they spoke not love
For me.

Oh, yesterday,
When love was young,
And I was fancy free,
Youth and hope were
Everywhere,
And the girls all smiled
At me.

Oh, yesterday,
I sat alone,
And felt the world grow cold,
A young girl smiled,
But not for me,
And now am I grown old.

OH, JENNY, SHE LOVED ME

Oh, Jenny, she loved me,
But I played the waiting game.
Now Jenny's gone, and I am old,
And love, it never came.

SWEET MARIE

Oh, sweet Marie once said to me,
When I said that we should part,
"You will not find a love like mine,
For I love with all my heart.
And though I am but rather plain,
And have no wit or complex brain,
All I have is yours to gain,
A love as pure as summer rain."

But I was young and could not see
The truth in what she said to me,
And being young, I played the part,
And left her with a broken heart,
But though I searched throughout
    the years,
I found not joy, but bitter tears,
And now I'd give the world to gain,
A love as pure as summer rain.

OH, MY DARLING LITTLE GIRL

Oh, my darling little girl,
    playing in the sun,
Will you shed a tiny tear
    before the day is done?
And will a naughty little bird
    whisper in your ear,
That the rainbow in your summer sky
    will shortly disappear,
That you'll fall down and scrape your knee,
    that pain will come to you,
That summer skies will darken
    and lose their summer blue,
That darkness and loneliness,
    and pain will come to you,
That the world is not a meadow,
    and our joys are short and few,
And someday soon (oh, Lord, too soon),
    a thief will steal your youth,
For, oh, my darling little girl,
    that birdy speaks the truth.
But do not cry, my little one,
    keep playing in the sun,
For childhood is a precious time,
    and soon the day is done.

ALAS, THAT TIME HAS COME TO ME

Alas, that time has come to me
When love is but a memory,
And all the hopes of springtimes past
Lie withered neath the winter's blast,
But still I dream the dreams of youth,
Embittered now by bitter truth,
And dream a dream of golden girls,
Of wine-red lips and tossing curls,
Of silver laughter and sparkling eyes,
Of love's embrace and lovers' sighs.
And so into my dreams they glide
To tease my heart, then quickly hide,
But while I dream, they come to me,
If only in a memory.

THE SAND IS FALLING IN THE GLASS

The sand is falling in the glass,
Falling as the hours pass,
And as I watch the pale moon climb,
I sense that there will come a time
When I will hear the owl's call,
And know the sand has ceased to fall.

A VERY LONG TIME AGO

I was thinking about your hair today
And the way you wore it on our wedding day,
A very long time ago.

It was full of curls and soft as down
And it shone in the sun a honey brown,
A very long time ago.

And though your hair's now silver-gray,
I'll say again what I said that day,
A very long time ago.

That I'll always love you, come what may,
And I love you now as I did that day,
A very long time ago.

YOU AND ME

The mystery of life is a secret,
    and ever will it be,
But the mystery of love is simple,
    it's simply you and me.

Oh, the future's a tightly held secret,
    that only the gods can see,
But the secret of love is simple,
    it's simply you and me.

MIRROR IMAGE

Oh, mirror image, you have aged,
The hollow cheeks, the thinning hair,
You will not lie to save me pain,
You show me what is really there.

Your eyes are sunken, with bags below,
Your skin is wrinkled and sallow,
Your nose is swollen and heavily veined,
Your teeth are broken and yellow.

How can you show me such a face,
All lies are not the same,
Must you now reveal the truth,
Am I or you to blame?

You've been a friend for all these years,
I've understood your pride,
Why have you now succumbed to truth,
Your age you do not hide.

Oh, mirror image, it breaks my heart,
Now the awful truth is told,
Yes, it breaks my heart to see you there,
Oh, Lord, you've grown so old!

"POOR OLD THING . . ."

They sat in brightly colored summer
  dresses beneath a large yellow and
  white umbrella at a small glass and
  wrought iron table out on the verandah
  of the Kensington Hotel, where, surrounded
  by the bright midday sun and countless
  pink and yellow roses and large masses
  of pale violet lilacs, they sipped cold
  lemonade, and talked and laughed,
  and shared little secrets and gossip, their
  eyes and smiles expressing surprise
  and delight, and they laughed and lifted
  their glasses so that rings and
  bracelets glinted and sparkled in the
  sun, while their voices and laughter,
  so full of youthful merriment,
  bubbled along like a sparkling
  brook across a green and flower-
  filled meadow.

The air was heavy with the sweet perfume
  of the many flowers and shrubs that
  grew along the outer edge of the thick
  green lawn that surrounded the
  sun-filled verandah, and while the
  sun was warm, a light breeze
  blew gently across the balcony and
  felt cool on their bare arms; the
  breeze also carried along the faint
  strains of a lilting waltz that floated
  out from the hotel ballroom through

the large glass doors that opened
onto the verandah — all of which
combined to intensify the loveliness
of the moment: the brilliant sunshine,
the cool tart taste of the lemonade, the
sweet scent and lovely colors of
the countless flowers and shrubs,
the lovely music, the cooling breeze,
and, most of all, the presence — the
smiling, joyous, loving presence —
of best friends, with their pretty
summer dresses, their lovely faces,
their warm and eager smiles, the
sound of their voices, their laughter . . .
lovely Clarissa, dearest Evelyn, and
the shiningly beautiful Margaret Ann . . .
three lovely flowers in full bloom,
here on the verandah, in the midday
sun, at the Kensington Hotel, laughing
and sipping lemonade, looking so
beautiful, so young, so full of
life, so . . .

And then, quite suddenly, in an instant,
    she came awake . . . came back from
    where she was . . . from that lovely
    summer afternoon . . . when they sat
    on the verandah . . . sipping lemonade . . .
    at the Kensington Hotel . . . to the present . . .
    here at the Sunshine Nursing Home . . . .

"There, now, that's a good girl . . . . Just one
   more teaspoon and we're all done . . . .
   There you go . . . . Oops! . . . Try not to
   shake so, dearie, you'll get your
   nice clean dress all messy . . . and
   we wouldn't want that, now, would
   we . . . ?"

"How's the old biddy doing?"

"Oh, it depends . . . she has her moments . . . .
   One minute she's here, and the next
   minute . . . . Well, who knows where
   she is? But, for an old gal of 87 . . . .
   Well, what can you expect . . . ? Messes
   herself, of course . . . ."

"She's a bit daffy, if you ask me . . . . Don't
   think she knows where she is half
   the time . . . . Lord knows what she's
   thinking . . . ."

"Oh, I don't suppose she's thinking much
   of anything . . . . My Auntie had a stroke,
   you know . . . couldn't say a word . . .
   just sat there like a mummy . . .
   poor old thing . . . ."

DO NOT THINK ABOUT THE WINTER

Do not think about the winter
And the pain of growing old,
Just think about our love, dear,
And the joy that it can hold.

Do not think about the winter
And of all the sorrows there,
Just think about our love, dear,
And this moment that we share.

Oh, do not fear the winter
And the parting it must bring,
For when we're in each other's arms,
It is forever spring.

OF ALL LIFE'S TREASURES

Of all life's treasures I would miss,
If I should cease to be,
Would not be power, glory, or gold,
But one sweet kiss from thee.

Yes, of all life's treasures I would choose,
If the choice were given me,
Would not be power, glory, or gold,
But one sweet kiss from thee.

DEEP IN THE STILL AND SILENT NIGHT

Deep in the still and silent night,
Beneath the moon's reflected light,
I dream that you are standing there,
With silver moonlight in your hair.

And on your cheek, a single tear,
And from your lips, the words I fear,
That tell me what I would not hear,
The time to part is drawing near.

And though you sigh, you will not tell
What mortal wound our love befell,
But in your eyes, where sorrows dwell,
I see a look that speaks farewell.

And on your breath, a lover's sigh,
But in your eyes, no reason why
A love like ours should come to die,
And on your lips, a kiss good-bye.

But still I say a prayer each night,
That when I see the moon's pale light,
That I will dream you're standing there,
With silver moonlight in your hair.

AND NOW, THERE SHE SAT

I looked at the face in the photograph
and was startled . . . the young girl that
looked back was astonishingly
pretty. And yet, when I looked at the
living woman, it was difficult to
imagine her at that age, a girl/woman,
when the sweet, wide-eyed innocence
and expectancy of youth was inseparable
from the knowing sensuousness that
sat in the corner of her smile and slipped
like a silken gown over her shoulders,
her arms, her breasts, her thighs — when
her hair, which could be worn down,
in thick brown ringlets that bounced
with each joyous, youthful step, and
shone like honey in the sun, or up,
which gave her a regal look and the
self-assured sophistication of a Park
Avenue debutante — when her eyes
showed both innocent delight and
knowing pleasure at a compliment —
when her laugh was like the ringing of
silver bells and her voice had the
bubbling sensuousness of champagne —
when her touch had all the accidental
good humor and pratfalls of youth and

the lingering caress of a lover — when her
movements (the way she walked, the
way she sat, the way she crossed her
legs) spoke of both the awkwardness
and unstudied innocence of youth and
the instinctive feline sensuousness
of a lioness in heat.

And now, there she sat, with a woolen shawl
around her thin shoulders, that seemed
to bend forward under its weight; her
eyes were small and watery; her face,
wrinkled and hollow-cheeked; her hair,
dull gray and thin; her chest, flattened and
hollowed out; her arms, thin and covered
with loose, finely wrinkled skin; her
fingers, boney and gnarled with
arthritis, and her voice (she spoke
very infrequently), thin and raspy —
all sadly reflective of her 87 years . . . .

And yet, every so often, when something
stirred in her memory, or when the light
struck her face at just the right angle,
there was a momentary hint of the
lovely young girl that used to live
in those old bones.

AND YET, THE NIGHT WILL SURELY COME

So much depends on the green meadow
Along the slope of this slow rising hill,
Covered by a great sweep of purple
Heather and golden daffodil.

And there's a sweetness in the air,
The perfumed scent of wildflowers,
    yellow, pink, and blue,
And the warmth of a summer's sun,
Glistening on droplets of morning dew.

And, above it all, an endless expanse
Of blue sky, filled with great billowing
    clouds of white,
While, here and there, upon the meadow,
Silent flutterings of yellow butterflies,
    so delicate and light.

Oh, so much depends on this fragile
    and fleeting moment,
That fills my heart with joy and peace,
And yet, the night will surely come,
Slowly, and steadily, and will not cease.

THERE IS A MOMENT

There is a moment,
  just before the sun sets,
Before the last remnant
  of glowing golden light
Slips slowly out of sight
  beneath the dark shroud of night,
When I wonder if this is the end
  of the light,
And the beginning of a night
  without end.

And it is just that thought,
  however fleeting,
That makes the rising of the sun
  on the following morning
So surprising, so welcome,
  so life-affirming.

And yet, as evening approaches,
  just before the sun sets,
There is a moment . . . .

ALONE

Alone, in the dark cold silence of evening,
Beside the faintly glowing embers
Of a dying fire, I sit and listen
For the half-remembered sound of her voice,
And see, as if in a dream,
The sweet sadness of her smile
And the calm blue soul of her eyes —
Brief moments of sunlight, warm and alive,
Amid the lengthening shadows
Of the oncoming night.

DUSK

Pink glows softly in a brown mist.
Oh, for a touch of blue.
But this is the quiet time,
And even white must gray,
And pink glow softly in a brown mist.

V
DUST

NO MATTER

No matter how moving the sunrise,
No matter how lovely the light,
No matter how fragrant the flower,
The day must give way to the night.

No matter how thrilling the story,
No matter how joyful the tune,
No matter how sweetly the bird sings,
The sun must give way to the moon.

No matter how haunting your beauty,
No matter what prayers you recite,
No matter how dearly I love you,
The day must give way to the night.

No matter what dreams of the future,
No matter how late or soon,
No matter what joys or sorrows,
The sun must give way to the moon.

No matter how many bright angels
Can dance on the point of a pin,
No matter how wise or foolish,
Over death no mortal can win.

I THINK OF YOU

I think of you in the spring,
when, on a sun-filled afternoon by the
lake, a sudden rain begins to fall,
and I watch two young lovers run,
hand in hand, toward the white
gazebo in the park, where, laughing,
and with wet hair and wet lips, they kiss.
And I think of you.

I think of you in summer,
when the first daisies uncurl their
bright burst of petals and stare at the
sun in startled delight, and I watch
a young couple walk by, and they
pause, and he places a daisy in her hair,
and they kiss.
And I think of you.

I think of you in autumn,
when I walk alone down a winding
country road, and the sky is slate gray,
and there is a sharp chill in the air and
a wisp of distant smoke from mounds
of burning leaves, and I spy a solitary
bird flying across a dark brown field
filled with endless rows of dry yellow
stubble, and my loneliness consumes me.
And I think of you.

I think of you in winter,
    when, in the gray light of dawn, I see
    the first snowflakes float by my window,
    and the house is still and filled with
    sleep, and I curl deeper into the thick
    blue quilt that still holds a faint trace
    of your perfume, and I almost feel you
    warm beside me.
    And I think of you.

Oh, my darling, I think of you
    in every season and in everything I see
    and hear and feel, and when the year has
    turned, and the first buds and blossoms
    of spring appear through the melting snow,
    I will miss you — and think of you —
    all over again — for another year.

THE PROMISE OF THE DAWN HAS FLED

The promise of the dawn has fled,
And summer's rose is almost dead,
And o'er the sky the night has spread,
And shadows fill my lonely bed,
And in the dark my tears are shed,
And I am cold and filled with dread,
And though on hope I've often fed,
For man, to live, needs more than bread,
Hope, like summer's rose, is dead,
And so on tears I feed instead,
And in the end when all is said,
And all the gold has turned to lead,
And these sad lines no longer read,
Then will I lie among the dead,
   dry leaves of fall.

LOVE IS LIKE A FLOWER

"Love," she said,
  "is like a flower.
   Can you tell me why?"

"Indeed, I can," he sadly said,
  "both blossom,
  both fade,
  both die."

THE PERFECT CLOCK

The perfect clock . . .
It does not lie
It does not sigh
It does not stop to cry
It does not blink
It does not think
It cannot tell a lie
It does not scheme
It does not dream
It does not tell us why
It simply ticks . . . ticks . . . ticks . . .
Then tells us when
It's time to die.

DAY BY DAY

Day by day,
Time slips away,
And with it goes our youth.

Day by day,
Time slips away,
And death's the final truth.

BUT I CANNOT TELL YOU WHY

The midwife stood beside the bed
And heard the newborn cry.
"I know how babes are born," she said,
"But I cannot tell you why."

—

The doctor stood beside the bed
And heard the young man cry.
"I know that life brings pain," he said,
"But I cannot tell you why."

—

The nurse she stood beside the bed
And heard the old man cry.
"I know that all grow old," she said,
"But I cannot tell you why."

—

The priest he stood beside the grave
And heard the mourners cry.
"I know that all men die," he said,
"But I cannot tell you why."

AND SO DID HE

They came, they told themselves, out of love,
   and because it was the right thing — the
   expected thing — to do.

They came, they said, to comfort the old man,
   and they assembled themselves around
   his bed like visitors at a museum, viewing
   some strange and vaguely unpleasant
   specimen in a glass case.

When they spoke, they spoke cautiously,
   censuring themselves lest they inadvertently
   speak of the future — there was no future.

When they spoke, they spoke only of the past,
   of persons and events he had long since forgotten
   and to which he did not respond.

When they spoke, they spoke in voices reserved
   for funeral parlors, and for offering
   condolences to the relatives of the deceased.

And when it was not their turn to speak, they
   said silent prayers that even they could
   not hear — could not bear to hear — that
   he would not die until they had left.

And then, after a decent interval,
   they all went away . . . and so did he.

I'VE WATCHED THE SEASONS COME AND GO

I've watched the seasons come and go,
Years of sun and years of snow,
But now a winter grips the day,
A winter that has come to stay,
A dark gray winter with biting cold,
Whose icy winds say you are old,
And all about, the snow piles deep,
With a cold that finds you in your sleep,
And the snow piles deeper with each passing day,
Oh, here's a winter that has come to stay,
A freezing winter of cutting cold,
Whose icy winds say you are old.

Yes, I've watched the seasons come and go,
The warming sun, the blowing snow,
But now a winter rules the day,
A winter now that's come to stay,
A winter of ice and numbing cold,
Whose frigid winds cry you are old,
While all about the snow piles deep,
With a cold that steals into your sleep,
And the snow piles deeper with each passing day,
Oh, here's a winter that's come to stay,
Whose cutting winds cry and moan,
With a cold that cuts into the bone,
An iron winter of freezing cold,
That grips the heart when you are old.

MEMORIES

Memories, like roots in an old
   unweeded garden, run deep,
      and so do sorrows,
And so too does the memory of you,
   of the still haunting beauty of your face,
      of your voice, of your touch;
And the roots hold fast, though the
   once shining blossoms have faded,
      have withered, have died away,
But the memory of your face, of the lovely
   flower that blossomed in the sun,
      that perfumed the world with its presence,
Still clings to my heart, like roots,
   deep in the old unweeded garden
      of my mind.

THE MEMORY OF YOU

The beauty of a flower
Lives long in the mind,
Though the flower may die,
It leaves its beauty behind.

And like the fair flower
That bloomed for a day,
The memory of you
Will not fade away.

LIFE AND DEATH

Life

is

(slap!)

a

mosquito

(slap!)

in the

night

(slap!).

—

Death
lies
sleeping
in
the
sun

.

ROSES

Roses
Don't mind
Dying,
Not if they know
You're hoping they won't.

Not if they know
It will break
Your heart.

Roses
Are funny
That way.

Ever
Wonder
Why
Roses
Have
Thorns?

COURTSHIP AND MARRIAGE

Courtship is roses.
"What a lovely surprise!"
Marriage is ragweed
And watery eyes.

IN THE DARKENING GLOOM OF EVENING

In the darkening gloom of evening,
On a cold midwinter's eve,
I doze by a dying fire,
And from strands of memory weave
A scene of such sweet sorrow,
When last I saw her leave,
That I cry out in my slumber,
For to dream is but to grieve.
Still I long to dream her before me,
For it's then that I almost believe
That she'll stay and love me forever,
Though I know that dreams can deceive.
And so I doze by the fire,
In the gloom of a winter's eve,
And dream she'll appear before me,
And that she will never leave.

THE GAME OF LIFE

I played the game of life,
As the wheel of fortune spun.
I played the game of life . . .
    And won!

I played the game of life,
And watched as the dice were tossed.
I played the game of life . . .
    And lost!

WHAT IS MAN?

"Oh, tell me, Master, if you can,
What exactly is a man?
You have studied history,
And pondered many a mystery,
But can you tell me what is man?
Please tell me, Master, if you can.
Oh, what is the answer? What is he?
Is he what he seems to be?"

"No, my son, it is illusion,
For the study of man leads
To one conclusion:
That for all his striving,
And all his schemes,
Man is merely dust and dreams."

A MOST VALUABLE LESSON

"Yestereve, in the clear light of a full
    moon, here in the Royal Gardens
    of the Palace of Life, the Princess
    Cecilia knelt beside a bubbling
    brook and gently kissed a frog.
    It was a most valuable lesson."

"Pray tell, Master, what happened?"

"Nothing. Absolutely nothing."

THOUGH ONE BE A KING

Though one be a king
    and another a clown,
The hand of Fate
    strikes them equally down,
For 'king' and 'clown'
    are but a name,
To Fate, it seems,
    they're both the same,
And while in life
    the king commands,
Because he wears
    a golden crown,
He cannot stay
    the hand of Fate,
When Fate arrives
    to strike him down,
For the only difference
    between king and clown
Is that one wears bells
    and the other a crown,
And 'king' and 'clown'
    are but a name,
To Fate, it's clear,
    they're both the same.

OLD MEN

Old men walk with a stoop,
Bent over by the weight of their years,
And by all the tears they never cried,
And all the lies they ever lied,
And all the things they never tried,
And all the friends who went and died;
And by all they did and now regret,
On which their hearts and hopes were set,
And all they planned and all they schemed,
And all that failed of all they dreamed;
And by all the love they know they missed,
And all the lips they never kissed,
And all the days they can't recall,
Of when they stood so straight and tall;
And by all the times they broke their word,
And all the praise they never heard,
And all that failed and turned to dust,
And found they could no longer trust;
And now they know that life won't last,
And that the future's in the past,
And so they wend their weary way,
And there is nothing more to say,
Except to use their final breath
To say farewell and smile at Death.
Old men.

I MISS YOU SO

I miss you so,
Especially at twilight,
When the gray purple of evening
Darkens into deep shadows,
And the air is still,
And a sad silence settles over all,
And I am alone.
Oh, I miss you so.

I miss you so,
Especially at night,
When the sky is black and starless,
And the air is damp and cold,
And the moon glows with
A pale and sickly light,
And I am alone.
Oh, I miss you so.

I miss you so,
Especially in the morning,
When the sun fills our room
With a warm golden light,
And the cooing of doves can be heard
In the garden below our window,
And I am alone.
Oh, I miss you so.

I miss you so,
Especially in the heat of day,
When the world is filled with
The sounds and colors of life,
When the sky is wide and blue
And filled with sunlight,
And lovers walk hand in hand,
And I am alone.
Oh, I miss you so.

I miss you so,
Especially when I remember
Your smile, the sound of your voice,
The calm blue soul of your eyes,
The great cloud of golden hair that
Framed your face, the touch of
   your hand,
And I am alone.
Oh, I miss you so.

IN THE MERRY MONTH OF MAY

O, I gave my love a red, red rose
In the merry month of May,
But she to me a white rose gave,
And sent me on my way.

And so I prayed most earnestly
A prayer that lovers say,
And prayed she would a red rose send,
For red is passion's way.

But now the summer's come and gone
And winter's on its way,
And the red, red rose I gave my love
Has faded all away.

SHE LOVED ME, SHE SAID

She loved me, she said,
As I stole from her bed,
And softly she whispered my name.
She loved me, she said,
And I knew it was true,
But I played the waiting game.
And now, too late, I long for her,
And softly I whisper her name,
And wish I had not played the fool
That played the waiting game.

IF YOU WERE HERE

If you were here tonight,
I would lie beside you and watch you
while you slept, and I would listen to the
quiet music of your breathing.

I would hold you in my arms
and let the warmth of you enfold me,
and I would whisper your name.

I would kiss your eyelids and feel
the delicate fringe of your lashes
against my lips and I would smile.

I would lay my head upon your pillow and
feel your breath against my cheek, and
inhale the delicate perfume of your hair.

If you were here tonight,
I would pray that this quiet moment —
lying beside you — holding you in my
arms — watching you sleep — would
never end.

But you are gone,
And there is only the darkness, the
mindless ticking of the clock, the cold
stillness of the night, and my weeping.

Oh, if only you were here.

THE FIRST TIME I SAW YOU

When we are young, we know we will
    never grow old, and yet, when we do,
    we barely remember when, or how, it
    happened. And though I am now no
    longer young (If I am no longer young,
    am I old?), I can remember clearly the
    first time I saw you.

And I remember being surprised — almost
    startled — when you suddenly appeared,
    walking and laughing with a group of young
    girls, who seemed to find your presence —
    your astonishing beauty — entirely
    unremarkable, as though talking
    and laughing with an angel were as
    natural and as unsurprising as sunshine.

There was no fanfare, no formal announcement
    of your arrival, no stopping of time, no
    great burst of light. No. One minute you
    were not there — in a crowd of rushing,
    laughing, shouting teenagers — and then,
    remarkably, in the very same instant,
    there you were.

And while I said nothing (I'm not sure
    I could have spoken), I was overwhelmed by
    the indescribable beauty — the irresistible
    sweetness — of your face. And then,
    unexpectedly, our eyes met, and you
    smiled — and I forgot to breathe — and
    in that very moment, you changed the
    world — and I was in love.

And now (and I admit it), I am old (and, no,
    I can't remember when it happened), but,
    yes, I do remember, with absolute clarity,
    the very moment I fell in love — and I love
    you still — though now you are gone.
    But I'll be back soon. I'll try to visit often —
    every week if I can. I'm not driving anymore,
    but Robert said he would drive me down and
    pick me up after he makes his deliveries. It's
    nice here. And someday soon, I'll be able to stay.
    I'm glad we decided on Roselawn. It's a lovely
    cemetery. Don't you think?

MAI LING

I

Mai Ling's hair, like raven's wings,
Mai Ling's eyes, held secret things,
Mai Ling's lips, a bright red bow,
Mai Ling's touch, made flowers grow,
Mai Ling's voice, a silver bell,
Mai Ling's thoughts, she would not tell,
Mai Ling's laugh, she laughed at me,
Mai Ling's heart, a mystery.

II

Mai Ling was a perfumed flower
   blooming in the sun,
Mai Ling was a cooling breeze
   when the sultry day was done,
Mai Ling was a temple bell
   in the morning mist,
Mai Ling was a lover's sigh
   when her tender lips were kissed,
Mai Ling was a gentle rain
   that falls on a summer's day,
Mai Ling was a little bird
   that one day flew away.

SWAN QUEEN

And when the final tragic and triumphant
    notes cry out that, once again, love
    conquers all, and the music comes to a stop,
And when the last of the *pirouettes* and
    arabesques, the *jetés*, *fouettés*, and
    tours en l´air come to an end, and the
    Swan Queen lies dead in a circle of light,
And when the curtain falls and the applause
    fades and the last tear is wiped away
    and the audience leaves and dissolves
    into the night,
And when the musicians, and the conductor,
    and the stagehands, and the ticket taker,
    and the ushers, and the concessionaire,
    and the *Maitre de Ballet* all leave
    and are swallowed up by the city,
And when the stage lights go out and the
    theatre is dark and closed,
Then the hauntingly beautiful and tragic
    Swan Queen, danced by Tanja Taratova
    (*née* Natalie Bernstein), will fly away
    in a taxi to her small, stuffy room at the
    Lexington Hotel, where she'll remove her
    wig and false eyelashes, cold cream her face
    and wipe away her makeup, call room
    service for a chicken salad sandwich, a pot of
    tea, and some aspirin, and spend the next
    hour and a half soaking her feet.

BEING DEAD'S AN AWFUL BORE

They found him lying by the door,
Lying dead upon the floor,
He had hung his coat upon the rack,
And then he had a heart attack,
And now he's lying on a bed,
Without a thought within his head,
And soon they'll place him in a box,
Where time is still, there are no clocks,
And nowhere to go where he might be late,
And nothing more to anticipate,
Oh, its exactly what he thought before,
Being dead's an awful bore.

And then they'll place him in the ground,
Where all is silent, safe, and sound,
There is no place for him to go,
There's nothing that he needs to know,
Nothing there is false or true,
There's nothing that he needs to do,
And there is nothing there to fear,
And nothing to see and nothing to hear,
And nothing to write and nothing to read,
And nothing to follow and nothing to lead,
Oh, it's exactly what he thought before,
Being dead's an awful bore.

And when they place him in the ground,
They'll get a priest and gather round,
And then they'll cry and then they'll pray,
And he won't hear a thing they say,
And then he'll lie there all alone,
Just lying there, flesh and bone,
Where there's nothing to love and nothing to hate,
And you can't be early and you can't be late,
Where there's nothing to feel and nothing to dream,
And there's never a whisper and never a scream,
Yes, it's *exactly* what he thought before,
Being dead's an awful bore.

And that, it seems, is what we fear,
It's not the myths we tell and hear,
It's not the stories of Judgment Day,
Or the sadness when we pass away,
No, the truth is really a great deal worse,
Once we leave that shiny hearse,
Yes, life *is* full of grief and woe,
And what it means we cannot know,
But life is also full of *life*,
And *that*, in spite of all the strife,
Is what they've learned who've gone before,
Being dead's an awful bore!

AND YET . . .

Oh, love, I've tried so hard to forget,
But it's hard to let you go,
To forget how much I love you,
And that I miss you so.

And so I never think about
A face beyond compare,
The sweetest lips, the cutest nose,
And all that golden hair.

And I never, ever think about
The magic in your eyes,
Your funny grin, your dimpled chin,
And all those loving sighs.

And I never think about your laugh,
And the magic when we kissed,
And how you used to touch my face,
And all the love I've missed.

Oh, I never, ever think of you,
And try so hard to forget,
For I know it's best to let you go,
And yet . . . .

WHEN THE BELLS WILL TOLL FOR THEE

The cemetery clock sounds a stately chime
To gravely mark the passing time,
Which none can stop, day or night,
Though prayers and pleadings we recite.

The church bells toll a somber air
To call the living in to prayer,
They mark the passing of a soul,
But do not ask for whom they toll.

No, do not ask for whom they toll,
The future's not ours to see,
But a time will come when the bells will toll,
When the bells will toll for thee.

WINTER'S COME

The days are short,
The nights are long,
The owl sings his
Cheerless song.

Winter's come,
And winter's cold,
The days grow short,
And I grow old.

DUST

I came upon an ancient wall,
Overgrown with vines and roots,
Half hidden by leaning branches
And their leaves, the stones uneven,
Stained with moss, and crumbling into dust.

And in the stones, now fractured
And cracked with age, worn by wind,
And branches, and countless rains,
I saw the work of roughened hands,
And knew that they, like the wall itself,
Had turned to dust.

Thus, are we, like the wall,
Inexorably reclaimed,
And, like the stones,
Returned to dust.

Oh, love, it is not in walls, or even
In life itself, but only in this moment,
And in our love, that we can trust.
All else is fleeting.
All else is dust.

EPILOGUE

UPON THE BEACH
Night

I stood one night upon the beach,
Beneath a moonless sky,
And watched the rolling surf unfurl,
And felt the wind whip by.

And as I stood upon the beach,
I heard the grating roar
Of waves that rolled in from the sea
And crashed against the shore.

And out upon the blackened sea
The lights of ships passed by,
And I heard from somewhere in the night
The foghorn's mournful cry.

And then I felt the wind blow cold,
And rain began to fall,
And thunder joined the crashing waves,
And darkness covered all.

Dawn

I lay that night upon the beach,
Beside the blackened sea,
And heard the surf against the sand,
And felt the wind blow free.

And the wind blew hard, and the wind blew cold,
And the rain continued to fall,
And all the world seemed lost and old,
And darkness covered all.

And I wondered if, a world away,
The sun was shining bright,
Or if all the world was dark and cold,
And crying in the night.

But then along the far horizon,
The dawn burst forth from the sea,
And the sun's bright light soon filled the sky,
And the gulls were flying free.

And the morning sky was ablaze with light,
And the ocean was green and blue,
And the crashing surf was capped with white,
And the world seemed fresh and new.

About the Author

Harvey Hirsch is the author of the best-selling Christmas book, THE CRÈCHE OF KRAKOW, about which the critics have written:

"Authentic . . . poignant . . . uplifting . . . a delightful book . . . ."

— Deborah Vetter, *Cricket Magazine*

"An absolute gem!"

— Pat Collins, *WOR Radio, New York*

He is also the author of A HOME FOR TANDY, a popular children's book recently republished in the PLATT & MUNK TREASURY OF STORIES FOR CHILDREN, an anthology of classic fairy tales and other children's stories. A third book, BARBED WIRE AND OTHER POINTED REMARKS, is an insightful, humorous, and irreverent collection of original observations about the human condition. PALE MOON, which has been enthusiastically received by the critics, is his first book of poetry.

Hirsch, who is married and the father of four daughters, lives in Michigan, where he is currently at work on a second collection of poems, LOVE SONG, and a science fiction novel, THE SUN BETWEEN.